Summer
FIZZ

Summer FIZZ

OVER 100 RECIPES FOR REFRESHING SPARKLING DRINKS

RYLAND PETERS & SMALL
LONDON • NEW YORK

Senior Designer Toni Kay
Head of Production
  Patricia Harrington
Creative Director
  Leslie Harrington
Editorial Director Julia Charles
Indexer Hilary Bird

First published in 2022
by Ryland Peters & Small,
20–21 Jockey's Fields,
London WC1R 4BW
and
341 E 116th St,
New York NY 10029

www.rylandpeters.com

10 9 8 7 6 5 4 3 2 1

Recipe collection compiled by
Julia Charles. Recipes © copyright
Julia Charles, Jesse Estes, Mat Follas,
Laura Gladwin, Carol Hilker, Kathy
Kordalis, Louise Pickford, Ben Reed,
David T. Smith & Keli Rivers 2022.
Design and photographs © Ryland
Peters & Small 2022. See page 144
for full text and picture credits.

ISBN: 978-1-78879-437-4

A CIP record for this book is available from
the British Library.

US Library of Congress cataloging-
in-publication data has been
applied for.

Printed and bound in China.

NOTES

• Both metric and imperial oz/
US cups are included. Work with
one set of measurements and
do not alternate between the
two within a recipe. All spoon
measurements given are level:
1 teaspoon = 5 ml;
1 tablespoon = 15 ml.

• When a recipe calls for citrus
zest or peel, buy unwaxed fruit and
wash well before using. If you can
only find treated fruit, scrub well
in warm soapy water before using.

• To sterilize screw-top jars and
bottles to store syrups and cordials,
preheat the oven to 160°C/150°C
fan/325°F/ Gas 3. Wash the jars
and/or bottles and their lids in hot
soapy water then rinse but don't
dry them. Remove any rubber
seals, put the jars onto a baking
sheet and into the oven for 10
minutes. Soak the lids in boiling
water for a few minutes.

• Popaball Bursting Bubbles are
used in the cocktails on pages 28,
48 and 98, however, their inclusion
in recipes is optional. Visit
www.popaball.co.uk for more
information about the product.

Contents

Introduction

On a long, hot summer's day there is nothing more refreshing or satisfying than an ice-cold drink, and the addition of fizz makes these recipes the ultimate refreshing choice. Whether enjoyed during a relaxed evening in the garden as the heat of the day slips away, or in the blazing sunshine with a novel in hand, the long hours of summer deserve drinks with equal vibrance and excitement.

The summer months bring a wide range of events from poolside celebrations and boozy brunches to weddings and al fresco dinners. When hosting you may be searching to serve something as fun and fresh as these events themselves, going beyond beverages that can be served all year round. This collection of sparkling and delightful summer drinks will provide you with recipes that cater to all occasions and tastes. For the perfect accompaniment to a Sunday morning croissant with friends, you will find a whole chapter on Brunch Drinks, from the classic Mimosa to the less conventional Sunshine

Negroni. To kick off an evening meal by sunset, go for Sparkling Apéritifs such as the Coco Mango, or the delightfully delicate and floral Jasmine Blossom. For some great all-rounders, the Summer Cocktails chapter offers everything from a Sparkling Cosmopolitan to a Tequila Sparkler. For those extra hot days or evenings where the heat lingers and crickets chirp in the garden, try Spritzes & Coolers such as a Pineapple Sangria. On evenings where you are hosting a large crowd, Pitchers & Punches will provide the perfect way for you to please guests with ease; your family and friends will love Watermelon Fizzy Punch. Finally, for those abstaining from the booze on a hot afternoon who still want a refreshing tipple, head for Mocktails & Cordials such as Spiced Cream Soda and Citrus Fizz.

These fun and fizzy recipes come with easy-to-follow methods which require no specialist equipment. However, all at-home bartenders can benefit from a cocktail shaker and measuring jigger. Balloon (copa) glasses are good to have on hand for spritzes and gin and tonics, whilst flutes are great for brunch drinks or sparkling apéritifs. You may also want pitchers and punch bowls as they are ideal for serving a crowd. Wine glasses are also great all-rounders, and acrylic or bamboo drinking cups can provide an attractive way to serve fizzy cocktails without having to worry about breakages. You can also garnish these drinks in inventive and summery ways; throw in the fresh fruits that the summer months bring abundantly, or edible flowers and citrus slices. Novelty stirrers, paper straws and cocktail umbrellas can also be the perfect way to add the finishing touch to a sparkling summer beverage. And don't forget to have plenty of ice on hand!

We hope that you enjoy this lively cocktail collection and discover delicious ways to keep your mornings, afternoons and nights fizzing with excitement all summer long.

Brunch Drinks

Bellini

Mmmm, basking in the golden sunlight of a palazzo terrace in Venice, ice-cold Bellini in hand... If you're longing for an Italian summer, just serve these at your next brunch party. (Pictured left.)

35 ml/1½ oz good-quality, well-chilled peach juice

a dash of Chambord (optional)

well-chilled Prosecco, to top up

a fresh peach slice, to garnish

SERVES 1

Pour the peach juice into a cold flute glass and stir in the Chambord, if using. Half-fill with Prosecco and stir gently. Top up with more Prosecco, garnish with a small peach slice and serve at once.

Mimosa

Presenting the Bucks Fizz's much classier cousin from across the pond: the Mimosa, which is beautifully enhanced by a dash of Cointreau.

about 65 ml/2¾ oz well-chilled freshly squeezed orange juice

1 teaspoon Cointreau

about 65 ml/2¾ oz well-chilled Prosecco

SERVES 1

Half-fill a cold flute glass with the orange juice. Add the Cointreau and half the Prosecco. Stir gently, then add the rest and serve at once.

NOTE If you're making a tray of these, help the bubbles stay perky by adding half the Prosecco and stirring all the glasses. Finish off with the final dose of Prosecco just before serving.

Breakfast in Milan

Okay, so you don't have to wake up in Milan, but you'll definitely feel a little chic after enjoying one of these of a morning, along with a melt-in-the-mouth pastry. Continental breakfast in bed, anyone?

3 teaspoons shredless orange
   marmalade
15 ml/½ oz freshly squeezed
   lime juice
a dash of Campari (optional)
25 ml/1 oz gin
well-chilled Prosecco, to top up

SERVES 1

Put the marmalade in a cocktail shaker with the lime juice, Campari, if using, and gin. Half-fill the shaker with ice cubes and shake vigorously. Strain into a cold Martini glass and top up with Prosecco. Serve at once.

Pomini

The tartness of the grapefruit juice works well with the Champagne as a refreshing brunch cocktail. (Pictured left.)

300 ml/1¼ cups grapefruit
   juice
1 x 750-ml bottle well-chilled
   Champagne
1 small grapefruit, cut into
   6 small slices

SERVES 6

Divide the grapefruit juice between six flute glasses and top up with Champagne. Add a small slice of grapefruit to each glass and serve at once.

Mango Morning

This is a bright, tropical sunshine-filled alternative to the classic Mimosa (see page 11) or Buck's Fizz. You won't be able to help being in a good mood if you're handed one of these. (Pictured on page 8.)

15 ml/½ oz gin
50 ml/2 oz mango juice
1 teaspoon freshly squeezed
   lemon juice
well-chilled Cava, or other
   dry sparkling wine,
   to top up
a lemon zest twist, to garnish
   (optional)

SERVES 1

Pour the gin, mango juice and lemon juice into an ice-filled cocktail shaker and shake well. Strain into a chilled flute glass and top with Cava. Garnish with a lemon zest, if liked, and serve at once.

Sanguinello Fizz

This sophisticated sparkler celebrates all the sweet, tart and bitter qualities of blood oranges – the perfect accompaniment to your morning pancake stack!

40 ml/1¾ oz blood orange juice
1 teaspoon Campari
10 ml/⅓ oz limoncello
well-chilled Prosecco, or other
  dry sparkling wine, to top up
a blood orange slice, to garnish

SERVES 1

Pour the blood orange juice, Campari and limoncello into an ice-filled cocktail shaker and shake well. Strain into a chilled flute glass and top up with Prosecco. Garnish with a blood orange slice and serve at once.

Rosy Glow

Inspired by the classic cocktail Sex on the Beach, which was created in the 1980s – an era known for its provocatively named cocktails – this fruity concoction is dangerously drinkable so just have one!

10 ml/⅓ oz peach schnapps
10 ml/⅓ oz Chambord
15 ml/½ oz freshly squeezed
   orange juice
15 ml/½ oz cranberry juice
well-chilled Prosecco, or other
   dry sparkling wine, to top up
an orange zest, to garnish

SERVES 1

Pour the peach schnapps, Chambord, orange juice and cranberry juice into an ice-filled cocktail shaker and shake well. Strain into a chilled flute glass and top up with Prosecco. Garnish with an orange zest and serve at once.

Prosecco Mary

This is a delicious sparkling twist on the classic brunch drink, and popular cure-all, the Bloody Mary. Try it for a change, you may find you prefer it!

25 ml/1 oz vodka

75 ml/3 oz tomato juice

a dash of Tabasco or
   sriracha sauce

a pinch of sugar

a dash of smoked water
   (optional; available in
   supermarkets, and fun!)

about 75 ml/3 oz well-
   chilled Prosecco

cucumber slices and/or
   a celery stick, to garnish

SERVES 1

Put the vodka, tomato juice, Tabasco, sugar and smoked water, if using, into a cocktail shaker half-filled with ice cubes. Shake vigorously and pour, ice cubes and all, into a chilled collins glass.

Add half the Prosecco and stir gently to combine. Top up with the rest of the Prosecco, add some cucumber slices down the side of the glass (or a celery stick if you prefer) and serve at once with a straw and stirrer.

NOTE Smoked water is delicious but can overpower, so exercise caution and use no more than $1/4$ teaspoon to begin with.

Sunshine Negroni

A visually stunning and refreshingly juicy twist on a classic Negroni.

25 ml/³⁄₄ oz citrus-forward gin,
   such as Gordon's Sicilian
   Lemon Gin
25 ml/³⁄₄ oz Aperol
25 ml/³⁄₄ oz Dolin Blanc
10 ml/¹⁄₂ oz freshly squeezed
   orange juice
35 ml/1 oz grapefruit soda
1 teaspoon grenadine
orange slices, to garnish

SERVES 1

Add the gin, Aperol, vermouth and orange juice to an ice-filled highball glass and gently stir. Top up with chilled grapefruit soda and slowly pour the grenadine down the inside of the glass. Garnish with orange slices and serve at once.

NOTE Any grapefruit soda can be used here, even something like Lilt, but for the optimal visual effect it's best to use a white grapefruit soda such as Ting or San Pellegrino over a red grapefruit variety.

Sparkling
Apéritifs

Aviation Royale

Channel the 1920s Jazz Age with this sparkling variation on the classic Aviation cocktail. It's a sophisticated combination of gin and Maraschino liqueur, with a splash of crème de violette.

25 ml/1 oz gin
10 ml/¹/₃ oz freshly squeezed
    lemon juice
1¹/₂ teaspoons Maraschino
a dash of crème de violette
well-chilled Champagne, or
    other dry sparkling wine,
    to top up
a maraschino cherry, to garnish

SERVES 1

Pour the first four ingredients into an ice-filled cocktail shaker and stir well. Strain into a chilled flute glass and top up with Champagne. Garnish with a maraschino cherry and serve at once.

Rosebud

Feisty yet delicate, and strangely captivating... no, not a plucky romantic heroine, but a rather lovely gin-based summer apéritif.

1 teaspoon rose water
20 ml/³/₄ oz elderflower liqueur
15 ml/¹/₂ oz gin
1 teaspoon freshly squeezed
  lemon juice
well-chilled Prosecco, to top up
edible rose petals, to garnish (optional)

SERVES 1

Put the rose water, elderflower liqueur, gin and lemon juice in a cocktail shaker. Add a handful of ice and shake well. Strain into a chilled flute glass and top up with Prosecco. Garnish with a few rose petals and serve at once.

Raspberry Dazzler

Raspberry is shown off to its best advantage in this delectably fruity and intense vodka creation.

4 fresh raspberries, plus a few extra
¹/₂ teaspoon sugar
1 teaspoon Chambord
25 ml/1 oz vodka
1 teaspoon raspberry bursting bubbles
  (optional), see page 4
well-chilled Prosecco, to top up

SERVES 1

Put the 4 raspberries and sugar in a cocktail shaker and muddle well. Add the Chambord and vodka and a handful of ice cubes and shake well. Strain into a chilled flute glass and add the bursting bubbles, if using. Add half the Prosecco, stir gently, then add the rest, garnish with a few raspberries and serve at once.

Bello Marcello

Even the most committed whisky-phobe will love this refreshing summer sparkler. Try it and be surprised! (Pictured left.)

35 ml/1½ oz whisky
15 ml/½ oz Cointreau
well-chilled Prosecco,
  to top up
a strip of lemon zest,
  to garnish

SERVES 1

Pour the whisky and Cointreau into an old-fashioned glass filled with ice cubes. Stir well, then top up with Prosecco. Squeeze the lemon zest in half lengthways over the drink so that the essential oils in the skin spritz over it, then serve at once.

Beretta 18

An Italian take on a classic, the French 75. Both are named after World War I artillery and both are classy numbers – serve up one of these and impress your guests. (Pictured on page 24.)

25 ml/1 oz gin
15 ml/½ oz limoncello
well-chilled Prosecco,
  to top up
a strip of lemon zest,
  to garnish

SERVES 1

Put the gin and limoncello in a cocktail shaker or collins glass with a handful of ice cubes and stir until they are very cold. Strain into a chilled flute glass and top up with Prosecco. Squeeze the lemon zest in half lengthways over the drink so that the essential oils in the skin spritz over it, then drop it in and serve at once.

Jasmine Blossom

The beautiful floral perfume of jasmine tea, given a little backbone by a dash of gin and the almond scent of orgeat, makes this an unusual but delightful daytime cocktail that will intrigue your guests.

35 ml/1¹/₂ oz freshly made strong
   jasmine tea, chilled
1 teaspoon orgeat syrup
10 ml/¹/₃ oz gin
well-chilled Asti Spumante,
   or other semi-sweet sparkling
   wine, to top up
jasmine leaves or blossoms,
   to garnish (optional)

SERVES 1

Pour the chilled jasmine tea, orgeat syrup and gin into an ice-filled cocktail shaker and shake well. Strain into a chilled flute glass and top up with Asti. Garnish with jasmine, if liked, and serve at once.

Petal

This is an elegant drink, both in appearance and flavour, with a delicate, rose-scented perfume that's reminiscent of Turkish delight.

1 large strawberry, hulled
25 ml/³/₄ oz sugar syrup
10 ml/¹/₄ oz freshly squeezed lime juice
10 ml/¹/₄ oz rose water
100 ml/3 oz well-chilled dry sparkling
  rosé wine
edible rose petals, to garnish

SERVES 1

In a shaker, lightly muddle the strawberry and sugar syrup. Once pulped, add the lime juice and rose water and shake for a few seconds. Strain into an ice-filled old-fashioned glass and top up with sparkling rosé. Garnish with rose petals and serve at once.

Lavender Rosé Royale

This gin-based delight is similar to a French 75 in style with the lavender syrup just giving it a subtle floral note.

2 large strawberries, hulled
60 ml/2 oz floral gin
15 ml/¹/₂ oz freshly squeezed
  lemon juice
15 ml/¹/₂ oz Monin lavender syrup
200 ml/³/₄–1 cup well-chilled extra-dry
  sparkling rosé wine
edible flowers, to garnish

SERVES 2

Put the strawberries into a cocktail shaker and muddle with a muddler or the end of a wooden rolling pin. Once pulped, add the gin, lemon juice, lavender syrup and 4–5 ice cubes. Shake until chilled, about 20 seconds. Strain the mixture into two coupe glasses and top up with sparkling rosé. Garnish with edible flowers and serve at once.

Pom Pom

Traditionally used in a Harvey Wallbanger, here Galliano's vanilla-anise and herby notes really enhance the pomegranate.

10 ml/¹/₄ oz Galliano
40 ml/1¹/₂ oz pomegranate juice
well-chilled dry sparkling rosé wine,
    to top up
a few pomegranate seeds and a sprig
    of fresh mint, to garnish

SERVES 1

Pour the Galliano and pomegranate juice into a flute glass and top up with sparkling rosé. Garnish with a few pomegranate seeds and a sprig of mint. Serve at once.

Hibiscus Fizz

Hibiscus flowers have a delicious raspberry and rhubarb flavour that pairs with the berry fruit notes of rosé wine. Also added here is a splash of Lillet (see page 43) to balance the sweetness and bring a little more depth to the drink.

1 wild hibiscus flower, from a jar of
    flowers in syrup
2–3 teaspoons Monin hibiscus syrup
    (or use the syrup from the jar of
    hibiscus flowers if there is enough)
40 ml/1¹/₂ oz Lillet or white vermouth
well-chilled sparkling rosé wine,
    to top up

SERVES 1

Put a hibiscus flower in the bottom of a wide-necked coupe or Martini glass (with the petals reaching upwards). Gently pour in the hibiscus syrup and Lillet and top up with sparkling rosé wine. Serve at once.

Liaison Dangereuse

This lethal but seductive combination of bourbon, orange liqueur and Amaretto, lifted with a luxurious spritz of Champagne, would make a decadent finale for an al fresco meal. (Pictured left.)

15 ml/¹⁄₃ oz bourbon

well-chilled Champagne,
   or other

10 ml/¹⁄₃ oz Cointreau

dry sparkling wine, to top up

1 teaspoon amaretto

an orange zest twist,
   to garnish (optional)

SERVES 1

Pour the first three ingredients into an ice-filled cocktail shaker and stir well. Strain into a chilled flute glass and top up with sparkling wine. Garnish with an orange zest, if liked, and serve at once.

Appleblack

The perfect choice for a sophisticated summer soirée, the Appleblack offers a more potent and conversation-starting alternative to the ever-popular Kir Royale. (Pictured on page 1.)

15 ml/¹⁄₂ oz Calvados

15 ml/¹⁄₂ oz crème de cassis

well-chilled Crémant de
   Loire, or other dry
   sparkling white wine,
   to top up

SERVES 1

Pour the Calvados and crème de cassis into an ice-filled cocktail shaker and stir well. Strain into a chilled flute glass, top up with Crémant and serve at once.

Coco Mango

This sparkling taste of the tropics is a lot lighter and more quaffable than some heavy coconut-based, tiki-style drinks.

15 ml/½ oz coconut rum,
 such as Malibu
15 ml/½ oz gin
25 ml/1 oz mango juice
10 ml/⅓ oz freshly squeezed
 lime juice
a dash of Angostura bitters
 (optional)
well-chilled Asti Spumante, or
 other semi-sweet sparkling
 wine, to top up
a dried mango strip, to garnish
 (optional)

SERVES 1

Pour the first five ingredients into an ice-filled cocktail shaker and shake well. Strain into a chilled flute glass and top up with Asti Spumante. Garnish with a strip of dried mango, if liked, and serve at once.

Lillet de Loire

Lillet is a delicious perfumed aperitif wine made in Bordeaux, France, made famous by James Bond and the Vesper Martini. Combined with French dry sparkling wine and sharpened with lemon, it makes the perfect simple pre-dinner drink.

50 ml/2 oz Lillet
a dash of freshly squeezed lemon juice
well-chilled Crémant de Loire, or
other dry sparkling wine, to top up

SERVES 1

Pour the Lillet and lemon juice into an ice-filled cocktail shaker. Stir well and strain into a chilled cocktail glass. Top up with Crémant and serve at once.

Posy

Blossomy scents abound, but never fear – this is far subtler than perfume. Its semi-dry and refined blend of floral flavours will win over any cocktail aficionado.

1 teaspoon crème de violette
10 ml/¹⁄₃ oz elderflower liqueur
5–10 ml/1 teaspoon–¹⁄₃ oz grenadine,
**   to taste**
a dash of freshly squeezed lemon juice
well-chilled Crémant de Loire, or other
**   dry sparkling wine, to top up**
an edible flower, to garnish (optional)

SERVES 1

Pour the first four ingredients into an ice-filled cocktail shaker and stir well. Strain into a chilled flute glass and top up with Crémant. Garnish with an edible flower, if liked, and serve at once.

Summer
Cocktails

Ultra Violet

Try out this subtly floral delight at your next drinks party and you'll be rewarded with plenty of oohs and aahs, not least because of it's fabulously summery aquamarine colour.

25 ml/1 oz gin
20 ml/³/₄ oz crème de violette
10 ml/¹/₄ oz blue curaçao
10 ml/¹/₄ oz freshly squeezed
   lemon juice
well-chilled Prosecco, to top up
a lemon zest and edible flower,
   to garnish

SERVES 1

Put the gin, crème de violette, blue curaçao and lemon juice in a cocktail shaker and add a handful of ice cubes. Shake well, then strain into a chilled Martini or cocktail glass. Top up with Prosecco, garnish with a lemon zest and an edible flower and serve at once.

Cherry Baby

Bakewell tart in a glass, you say? Yes please! Lovers of cherry and almond flavours everywhere will be delighted with this.

25 ml/1 oz amaretto

15 ml/¹/₂ oz cherry brandy

25 ml/1 oz syrup from a jar of maraschino cherries

1 teaspoon cherry bursting bubbles (optional), see page 4

well-chilled Prosecco, to top up

maraschino cherries, to garnish

SERVES 1

Put the amaretto, cherry brandy and syrup in a cocktail shaker and add a handful of ice cubes. Shake well, then strain into an old-fashioned glass. Add the bursting bubbles, if using, then top up with Prosecco. Serve at once.

Stiletto

This is simple but deliciously refreshing, and just like its namesake, adding one to your next soirée will definitely make a fashion statement.

25 ml/1 oz amaretto

15 ml/¹/₂ oz freshly squeezed lime juice

well-chilled Prosecco, to top up

lime slice, to garnish

SERVES 1

Put the amaretto and lime juice in a cocktail shaker with a handful of ice cubes and shake well. Strain into a chilled coupe glass and top up with Prosecco. garnish with a thin slice of lime and serve at once.

Sparkling Manhattan

If you love Manhattans but sometimes find them a bit rich, you'll love this. This is based on a Sweet Manhattan, but feel free to switch the sweet vermouth for dry if you prefer yours dry – or use half sweet and half dry vermouth if you're more of a Perfect Manhattan fan.

15 ml/½ oz bourbon
10 ml/⅓ oz sweet red vermouth
a dash of Angostura bitters
1 teaspoon Maraschino (optional)
well-chilled Champagne,
    to top up
maraschino cherries, to garnish

SERVES 1

Pour the first four ingredients into an ice-filled cocktail shaker and stir well. Strain into an ice-filled old-fashioned glass and top up with Champagne. Garnish with maraschino cherries and serve at once.

Classic Champagne Cocktail

This, the original sparkling cocktail, dates back to the mid-19th century. Cognac was the spirit of choice, but Grand Marnier adds a pleasant citrus note. Only Champagne will do here – you need its toasty, biscuity flavours. (Pictured right.)

1 brown sugar cube
several dashes of Angostura bitters
25 ml/1 oz cognac or Grand Marnier,
   or a mixture of the two
well-chilled Champagne, to top up

SERVES 1

Coat the sugar cube with Angostura bitters and drop it into a chilled flute glass. Chill the cognac and/or Grand Marnier in a separate glass by stirring it gently with ice cubes, then strain it into the flute. Top up with Champagne and serve at once.

The Metropolis

Perhaps inspired by the Parisian café classic Kir Royale, the Metropolis combines sparkling wine with the same appealing berry flavours, but adds a kick of vodka to give it a steely edge.

25 ml/1 oz vodka
25 ml/1 oz crème de framboise
well-chilled Crémant de Bourgogne,
   or other dry sparkling wine, to top up

MAKES 1

Fill a cocktail shaker with ice cubes and add the vodka and crème de framboise. Shake well and strain into a chilled flute or cocktail glass. Top up with Crémant and serve at once.

Lavender French 75

The epitome of elegance, a French 75 is the perfect apéritif for almost any occasion. Gin, Champagne, lemon juice and sugar syrup – so simple but so effective. This floral twist adds just a hint of perfume, barely there but enough to transport you to the lavender fields of Provence. (Pictured left.)

50 ml/2 oz gin
30 ml/1 oz freshly squeezed
    lemon juice
20 ml/¹/₂ oz Monin lavender syrup
well-chilled Champagne or any
    Crémant, to top up
lemon twists, to garnish

SERVES 2

Pour the gin, lemon juice and lavender syrup into a cocktail shaker filled with ice cubes. Shake until frosted then strain the mixture into a small jug/pitcher and divide between two flute glasses. Top up each one with Champagne or Crémant. Garnish each with a lemon twist and serve at once.

Jalisco Flower

Tequila fans will be wowed by this classy combination, which adds up to so much more than the sum of its parts. (Pictured on page 44.)

15 ml/¹/₂ oz tequila
20 ml/³/₄ oz elderflower liqueur
35 ml/1¹/₂ oz pink grapefruit juice
well-chilled Prosecco, to top up
edible flower, such as nasturtium
    or violet, to garnish

SERVES 1

Put the tequila, elderflower liqueur and pink grapefruit juice in a cocktail shaker and add a handful of ice cubes. Shake well and strain into a chilled coupe glass. Top up with Prosecco, garnish with an edible flower and serve at once.

Original Sin

This cocktail is a testament to just how well tequila and sparkling wine or Champagne can pair. The enticing combination of fresh apple, mint and elderflower liqueur means that this drink is always a crowd-pleaser.

1/4 Granny Smith apple, cubed

6–8 fresh mint leaves, plus a mint
   sprig to garnish

25 ml/3/4 oz calle 23 blanco tequila

20 ml/2/3 oz freshly squeezed lime juice

15 ml/1/2 oz elderflower liqueur

10 ml/2 teaspoons sugar syrup

well-chilled sparkling white wine,
   to top up

Muddle the apple cubes and mint leaves in the base of a cocktail shaker. Add all the other drink ingredients, except the Champagne, to the shaker with cubed ice. Shake and then double strain into a flute glass. Top up with sparkling wine, garnish with a mint sprig and serve at once.

SERVES 1

Mexican 55

While this drink was originally created by Tomas Estes, in 1988, the specific recipe featured here was adapted by Glenn Morgan at Lab Bar in London.

25 ml/3/4 oz silver tequila

15 ml/1/2 oz freshly squeezed lime juice

1 teaspoon runny honey

10 ml/2 teaspoons yellow chartreuse

a dash of Bitter Truth Pimento Dram

a dash of Peychaud's Bitters

well-chilled Champagne, to top up

a pared lime zest, to garnish

Shake all the drink ingredients, except the Champagne, in a cocktail shaker with ice cubes. Double strain into a chilled flute glass. Top up with Champagne, garnish with a pared lime zest and serve at once.

SERVES 1

Under the Volcano

This cocktail is smooth and refreshing on a hot day but be warned, it packs a strong punch! It features a simple homemade green tea syrup, but you could use a bottled one, such as Monin, if preferred.

25 ml/³/₄ oz green tea syrup (see below)
50 ml/1²/₃ oz mezcal
25 ml/³/₄ oz freshly squeezed lemon juice
3 dashes of absinthe
20 ml/²/₃ oz egg white
club soda, to top up
star anise, absinthe and lime zest, to garnish

SERVES 1

Add all the drink ingredients, except the club soda, to a cocktail shaker. Shake vigorously for 15–20 seconds, then single strain into a highball glass over cubed ice. Top up with club soda. For the garnish, soak a star anise in absinthe, carefully light on fire in a teaspoon and place over the top of strips of lime zest in the glass.

GREEN TEA SYRUP
Combine 2 tablespoons of loose-leaf tea (or 2 tea bags), 200 g/1 cup caster/superfine sugar and 230 ml/1 cup water in a saucepan. Bring to the boil, stirring frequently. Simmer for about 2 minutes. Remove from the heat, cover and stand for 2 minutes. Let cool before straining. Store for up to 1 week in a sealed bottle in the fridge.

Peach Blossom Spring

This is a slight deviation of the classic Bellini (see page 11), adding a little extra kick with the vodka and peach liqueur. Perfect for serving on a summer's evening or before a dinner party to get the night's proceedings off to a sophisticated start.

1 oz./25 ml vodka
1 oz./25 ml peach purée
2 teaspoons crème de pêche
well-chilled Prosecco, to top up
2 dashes of peach bitters
peach slices and a mint sprig,
   to garnish

SERVES 1

Add the vodka, peach purée and crème de pêche to a cocktail shaker filled with ice cubes and shake to mix. Strain into a flute glass, top up with Prosecco and add two dashes of peach bitters. Garnish with fresh peach slices and a mint sprig and serve at once.

La Paloma

Sour, sweet and salty, La Paloma gives the margarita a run for its money in Mexico. (Pictured left.)

60 ml/2 oz silver tequila

30 ml/1 oz freshly squeezed pink
   grapefruit juice

15 ml/^{1}/$_2$ oz freshly squeezed lime juice

^{1}/$_2$ tablespoon agave syrup

pink grapefruit soda or tonic, to top up

pink sea salt, for rimming the glasses

SERVES 1

First prepare the glass. Spread out some pink sea salt on a small saucer and add a little water to another. Dip the rim of the glass first into the water, then into the salt. Set aside. Pour the tequila, grapefruit juice, lime juice and agave syrup into an ice-filled cocktail shaker and shake until frosted. Strain into the salt-rimmed glass and serve at once.

Passion Star Martini

This combination of vanilla vodka and passionfruit has spread far from its origins in the early 2000s to be adopted (and adapted) by bars the world over and has become the star of the show! (Pictured on page 6.)

1 ripe passionfruit

30 ml/1 oz vanilla vodka

15 ml/^{1}/$_2$ oz Passoã (passionfruit liqueur)

^{1}/$_2$ tablespoon freshly squeezed lime juice

^{1}/$_2$ tablespoon sugar syrup

well-chilled Prosecco, to top up

SERVES 1

Halve the passionfruit and scoop the seeds into a cocktail shaker. Add the vodka, Passoã, lime juice and sugar syrup. Add a handful of ice cubes and shake vigorously. Strain into a Martini glass or coupe and top up with Prosecco. Garnish with the other passion fruit half and serve at once.

Singapore Sling

Created at the Raffles hotel in Singapore, when this drink is made correctly, and without using one of the cheap pre-mixes, it is the peak of sophistication! The original recipe has long been a subject of hot debate, but this simple one will not disappoint.

25 ml/1 oz gin
25 ml/1 oz cherry brandy
25 ml/1 oz Benedictine
50 ml/2 oz pinepple juice
25 ml/1 oz freshly squeezed
   lime juice
a dash of Angostura bitters
chilled club soda, to top up
lemon zest curl and maraschino
   cherry, to garnish

SERVES 1

Put the gin, cherry brandy, Benedictine, pineapple juice and lime juice in a mixing glass filled with ice cubes. Add the Angostura bitters and stir gently to chill. Pour into an ice-filled sling or highball glass and top up with club soda. Garnish with a lemon zest and a maraschino cherry and serve at once.

Tequila Sparkler

A slammer is a shot of tequila topped up with Champagne, covered with your hand and slammed down on the table to make the bubbles fizz up. Here's a slightly more sophisticated take. (Pictured left.)

25 ml/1 oz tequila
15 ml/¹/₂ oz freshly squeezed lime juice
1 teaspoon sugar syrup
well-chilled Cava, or other dry sparkling
    wine, to top up
lime wedge, to garnish

SERVES 1

Pour the first three ingredients into an ice-filled cocktail shaker and shake well. Strain into an ice-filled old-fashioned glass and top up with Cava. Garnish with a lime wedge and serve at once.

Mojito

The minty Mojito is arguably the world's most popular summer cocktail and with good reason. It is sure to be happily received by your summer garden or pool party guests.

2 teaspoons caster/granulated sugar
20 ml/²/₃ oz freshly squeezed lime juice
a handful of leaves from a bunch of fresh
    mint, plus a sprig to garnish
50 ml/2 oz white rum
chilled sparkling water or club soda
2 dashes of Angostura bitters (optional)

SERVES 1

Combine the sugar and lime juice in the bottom of a highball glass. Add the mint leaves and gently compress them with the back of a bar spoon to release their flavour, but without bruising them. Add the rum and fill the glass three-quarters full with ice cubes. Stir the mixture with a bar spoon, then top up with sparkling water or soda. Add the bitters if you prefer to cut the sweetness. Garnish with a mint sprig, add a straw and serve at once.

La Dolce Vita

They don't call this delicious cocktail la dolce vita ('the good life')
for nothing. It makes a brilliantly fresh and light summertime drink.

about 8 small seedless white grapes

1 teaspoon runny honey

30 ml/1 oz vodka

well-chilled Prosecco, to top up

a lemon zest, to garnish

SERVES 1

Put five of the grapes in a cocktail shaker
with the honey and muddle well until
they release their juice. Add the vodka
and half-fill the shaker with ice cubes.
Shake vigorously and strain into a chilled
Martini glass. Top up with Prosecco,
garnish with the reserved grapes and
a lemon zest, and serve at once.

Elderflower Cup

Add some sparkle to a summer celebration with this refreshing combination
of elderflower and Prosecco. The flower garnish adds a pretty touch.

**20 ml/²/₃ oz. St. Germain elderflower
liqueur, or elderflower cordial,
as preferred**

60 ml ml/2 oz vodka

1 teaspoon freshly squeezed lemon juice

well-chilled Prosecco, to top up

**edible flowers, such as violas,
to garnish (optional)**

SERVES 2

Combine the liqueur (or cordial), vodka
and lemon juice in a cocktail shaker. Add
a handful of ice cubes and shake until
frosted. Strain into two tumblers and
slowly top up with Prosecco. Garnish
each with a few edible flowers (if liked)
and serve at once.

Kentucky Cooler

We all know that bourbon works beautifully with mint in a julep. This is a longer, more refreshing version, lengthened with grapefruit, soda and a dash of bitters. Just add ice, a veranda and some sun, and enjoy!

30 ml/1 oz mint syrup (see below)
120 ml/4 oz bourbon
200 ml/7 oz pink grapefruit juice
a few dashes of Angostura bitters
50 ml/2 oz sparkling water or soda
2 fresh mint sprigs and citrus
   slices, to garnish

SERVES 2

Add the mint syrup to a medium-sized jug/pitcher, along with the bourbon, grapefruit juice and Angostura bitters and stir gently to mix. Add a handful of ice cubes and the citrus slices. Top up with the club soda and pour into two tall, ice-filled glasses. Garnish each glass with a mint sprig and serve at once.

MINT SYRUP
Put 200 g/1 cup caster/granulated sugar, 5 fresh mint sprigs and 125 ml/½ cup water in a saucepan set over low heat. Heat gently, stirring frequently, until the sugar has dissolved. Remove from the heat and leave to cool, then strain out the mint. The syrup will keep in an airtight jar in the fridge for up to 2 weeks.

Prima Donna

Simply combine a zesty Italian lemon liqueur with vodka, tangy pomegranate juice and chilled Prosecco, for an elegant and pretty summer drink.

25 ml/³/₄ oz vodka
15 ml/¹/₂ oz limoncello
25 ml/³/₄ oz pomegranate juice
well-chilled Prosecco, to top up
pomegranate seeds, to garnish
(optional)

SERVES 1

Put the vodka, limoncello and pomegranate juice in a cocktail shaker and add a handful of ice cubes. Shake sharply and strain into an ice-filled rocks glass or tumbler. Top up with Prosecco, garnish with pomegranate seeds (if liked) and serve at once.

Ouzo Sunrise

Sparkling azure seas, sugar-cube white houses with blue shutters and pink bourgainvillea tumbling over every doorway... a kind of paradise. You too can be transported to the Greek islands with an ouzo-based cocktail. (Pictured on page 5, bottom right.)

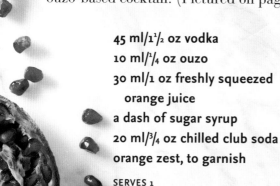

45 ml/1¹/₂ oz vodka
10 ml/¹/₄ oz ouzo
30 ml/1 oz freshly squeezed
   orange juice
a dash of sugar syrup
20 ml/³/₄ oz chilled club soda
orange zest, to garnish

SERVES 1

Add the vodka, ouzo, orange juice and sugar syrup to a cocktail shaker filled with ice. Shake until chilled, strain into a glass, top up with club soda to taste, garnish with an orange zest and serve at once.

Sparkling Cosmopolitan

This is a twist on the classic cosmopolitan. Adding sparkling wine turns it into a longer, more refreshing drink, ideal for summer gatherings. (Pictured left.)

45 ml/1½ oz vodka
15 ml/½ oz triple sec
15 ml/½ oz freshly squeezed
   lime juice
15 ml/½ oz cranberry juice
well-chilled Prosecco,
   to top up
a lime slice and fresh
   cranberries, to garnish

SERVES 1

Combine the vodka, triple sec, lime juice and cranberry juice in a cocktail shaker and add a handful of ice cubes. Shake until chilled. Strain into a rocks glass or tumbler and carefully top up with Prosecco. Garnish with a lime slice and a few fresh cranberries and serve at once.

Cosmo Royale

For a luxe spin, a float of Champagne is added here. The bubbles will happily sit on the surface if you pour them gently!

35 ml/1¼ oz lemon vodka
15 ml/½ oz freshly squeezed
   lime juice
15 ml/½ oz Cointreau
25 ml/1 oz cranberry juice
chilled Champagne, to float
an orange zest, to garnish

SERVES 1

Add all the ingredients, except the Champagne, to a cocktail shaker filled with ice cubes. Shake sharply and strain into a chilled Martini glass. Gently float the Champagne on the surface, garnish with an orange zest and serve at once.

Mediterranean Sparkle

The fresh scents of citrus and mint combine to make this sparkling cocktail the perfect drink for summertime sipping.

3 fresh mint leaves
45 ml/1½ oz vodka
25 ml/¾ oz triple sec
25 ml/¾ oz freshly squeezed
   lemon juice
1 teaspoon sugar syrup
chilled Cava, or other sparkling
   white wine, to top up

SERVES 1

Put 3 mint leaves in a cocktail shaker and muddle gently (do not bruise as this will make the drink bitter). Pour in the vodka, triple sec, lemon juice and sugar syrup. Add a handful of ice cubes and shake until frosted. Strain into a flute glass, top up with Cava and serve at once.

Spritzes
& Coolers

La Passeggiata

The passeggiata is an excellent Italian tradition of taking an evening stroll along a scenic strada, dressed up to the nines, to check out your neighbours. Why not give it a try in your neck of the woods, accompanied by one of these?

75 ml/3 oz chilled pink
   grapefruit juice
20 ml/³⁄₄ oz gin
20 ml/³⁄₄ oz Aperol
well-chilled Prosecco, to top up
a strip of grapefruit zest,
   to garnish (optional)

MAKES 1

Half-fill a collins glass with ice cubes. Add the pink grapefruit juice, gin and Aperol and stir well. Top up with Prosecco and stir very briefly. If you like, squeeze a strip of grapefruit zest over the top and drop it in. Serve at once.

Bourbon Spritz

Bright and fresh, this drink is the perfect pre-dinner tipple.

20 ml/^{2}/$_3$ oz bourbon
20 ml/^{2}/$_3$ oz fresh pink grapefruit juice
2 lemon wedges
5 ml/1 teaspoon Campari
75 ml/2^1/$_2$ oz Prosecco
50 ml/1^2/$_3$ oz club soda
fresh rosemary sprig and grapefruit
   zest, to garnish

SERVES 1

Combine all the drink ingredients in a large wine glass over ice cubes and stir gently for 5–10 seconds to combine. Garnish with a rosemary sprig and grapefruit zest and serve at once.

Marquee

Proof that bourbon can do long and fruity drinks too, this recipe was adapted from a cocktail created by Giovanni Burdi at Match Bar, London in 1998.

45 ml/1^1/$_2$ oz bourbon
45 ml/1^1/$_2$ oz cranberry juice
15 ml/^{1}/$_2$ oz Chambord
15 ml/^{1}/$_2$ oz freshly squeezed lemon juice
10 ml/2 teaspoons sugar syrup
3 fresh raspberries
10 ml/2 teaspoons egg white
a lemon zest and a fresh raspberry,
   to garnish

SERVES 1

Combine all the ingredients in a cocktail shaker and 'dry' shake first with no ice to emulsify the egg white. Add some ice cubes and shake hard. Strain into a highball glass over ice cubes, garnish with lemon zest and a raspberry and serve at once.

Viva España

Sangria with sparkling wine? Yes please! This is as refreshing as it is delicious. Switch the orange juice for blood orange or mandarin juice for delicious seasonal variations. (Pictured left.)

25 ml/1 oz Spanish red wine
15 ml/¹/₂ oz Dubonnet
25 ml/1 oz freshly squeezed
   orange juice
a dash of sugar syrup
well-chilled Cava, or any dry
   sparkling wine, to top up
an orange slice, to garnish

SERVES 1

Pour the first four ingredients into an ice-filled cocktail shaker and shake well. Strain into a chilled flute glass or small wine glass and top up with Cava. Garnish with an orange slice and serve at once.

Horse's Neck with a Kick

Dating back to the late 19th century, this drink was originally non-alcoholic and simply called a 'horse's neck'. Eventually, someone decided the drink was improved by adding bourbon and it became known as horse's neck 'with a kick'. It's simple, easy to make and very refreshing. (Pictured on page 78.)

60 ml/2 oz bourbon
3 dashes of Angostura bitters
ginger ale, to top up
a lemon zest, to garnish

SERVES 1

Combine all the ingredients in a highball glass over cubed ice. Stir for 5–10 seconds to combine the ingredients, chill and dilute the drink. Garnish with a long spiral of lemon zest and serve at once.

Bay Breeze

Pineapple adds a tropical touch to this variation on a Sea Breeze. Omit the pineapple, double the cranberry and add a lime wedge for a Cape Codder.

60 ml/2 oz vodka
45 ml/1½ oz fresh cranberry juice
75 ml/2½ oz fresh pineapple juice
chilled club soda, to top up
a pineapple wedge and leaf,
  to garnish (optional)

SERVES 1

Combine all the ingredients in a mixing glass filled with ice cubes. Stir to chill and pour into a highball glass filled with fresh ice cubes. Top up with a splash of soda for a lighter drink (if liked). Garnish with a pineapple wedge and leaf (if using) and serve at once.

Pineapple Sangria

This perfect summer cooler is loosely based on a Spanish sangria, in that it combines wine with fruit and a spirit base, in this case tasty pineapple vodka.

1 x 750-ml bottle fruity white wine
200 ml/6½ oz Smirnoff Pineapple Vodka
250 ml/1 cup fresh pineapple juice
125 ml/½ cup fresh orange juice, strained
about 250 ml/1 cup chilled club soda
lime slices, to garnish

SERVES 6

Combine the wine, vodka, pineapple juice and orange juice in a jug/pitcher and stir. Top up with the club soda and stir again. Pour into ice-filled rocks glasses or tumblers, garnish each glass with a lime slice and serve at once.

Negroni Bianco Bergamotto

The Italicus liqueur is flavoured with botanicals and the sparkling Prosecco adds a bright zing and liveliness to this stylish drink. (Pictured left.)

25 ml/³/₄ oz gin
25 ml/³/₄ oz Suze
25 ml/³/₄ oz Dolin Blanc
25 ml/³/₄ oz Italicus Rosolio
  di Bergamotto liqueur
well-chilled Prosecco, to top up
an orange wheel, to garnish

SERVES 1

Add the ingredients (except the Prosecco) to a large, ice-filled wine glass and gently stir. Top up with chilled Prosecco, garnish with an orange wheel and serve at once.

Newbie Negroni

This is designed to be a gentle introduction to the iconic classic, the Negroni, as it is both less sweet and less bitter. (Pictured on pages 2–3.)

25 ml/1 oz gin
25 ml/1 oz Pimm's No. 1 Cup
25 ml/1 oz red vermouth
15 ml/¹/₂ oz freshly squeezed
  orange juice
25 ml/1 oz club soda, or more to taste
lemon, lime and or orange zests,
  to garnish

SERVES 1

Add the ingredients to a large ice-filled wine glass and top up with chilled club soda. If the drink is still too strong, add more club soda. Garnish with lemon, lime and orange peels and serve at once.

Flavoured Gin & Tonics

It is easy to make flavour-infused gins at home with these simple recipes. To serve as a refreshing gin and tonic, allow 30 ml/1 oz of gin to 150 ml/5 oz good-quality tonic water, add ice cubes, garnish and enjoy.

RHUBARB GIN
150 g/5 oz fresh
  rhubarb
100 g/¹/₂ cup caster/
  superfine sugar
1 litre/4 cups gin
fresh mint, to serve
tonic water, to serve

CUCUMBER GIN
1 medium cucumber
table salt
1 litre/4 cups gin
fresh borage flowers
  and cucumber
  slices, to serve
tonic water, to serve

RED BERRY GIN
200 g/7 oz mixed
  berries
1 litre/4 cups gin
100 g/¹/₂ cup caster/
  superfine sugar
1 teaspoon rose water
lemon slices, to serve
tonic water, to serve

For each variation, clean then sterilize a 500-ml/2-cup clip-top jar, and its lid, by placing it in a preheated oven at 120°C (250°F) Gas ¹/₂ for at least 15 minutes before you add the ingredients.

RHUBARB GIN
Slice the rhubarb into even pieces about 1 cm/¹/₂ inch long, and place in the sterilized jar. Add the sugar, then fill with gin. Seal and leave to infuse for at least a couple of weeks. Agitate the jar gently every few days. After a couple of weeks, sample and add a little more sugar if needed. Serve garnished with a sprig of fresh mint.

CUCUMBER GIN
Clean the cucumber, then peel in even slices. Place the slices in the sterilized jar with a couple of large pinches of table salt, then fill with gin. Seal and leave to infuse for at least a couple of weeks. Agitate the jar gently every few days. After a couple of weeks, sample and add a little more salt if needed. Serve garnished with fresh borage flowers and a slice of cucumber.

RED BERRY GIN
Place the berries in the sterilized jar. Add the sugar to the jar, then fill with gin. Seal and leave to infuse for at least a couple of weeks. Agitate the jar gently every few days. After a couple of weeks, add the rose water and agitate to combine fully. Taste and add a little more sugar if needed. Serve garnished with a slice of lemon.

Porch-drinking Negroni

This laidback drink is just made for sipping on summer evenings. The muddled strawberries give it a soft, fruity note whilst the bitter lemon adds a refreshing crispness. (Pictured left.)

3 fresh strawberries
15 ml/³⁄₄ oz gin
10 ml/³⁄₄ oz Campari
10 ml/¹⁄₂ oz bianco vermouth
150 ml/5 oz bitter lemon
a mint sprig, to garnish

SERVES 1

Muddle (crush) the strawberries in the bottom of a rocks glass before adding the other ingredients and gently stirring. Add ice cubes, garnish with a mint sprig and serve at once.

The Negroni Cup

A longer version of the Porch-drinking Negroni (see recipe above), this can be served by the jug/pitcher so is ideal for patio parties.

75 ml/2¹⁄₂ oz gin
25 ml/1 oz red vermouth
25 ml/1 oz ginger wine
25 ml/1 oz Campari
450 ml/15 oz sparkling
   lemonade
lemon wheels and cucumber
   slices, to garnish

SERVES 4

Combine the ingredients (except the lemonade) in a large jug/ pitcher with ice and stir before garnishing with lemon wheels and cucumber slices. Top up with chilled lemonade, pour into ice-filled tumblers and serve at once.

B & B

Strawberries and basil are a flavour-pairing miracle, so bringing them together in a glass of pink fizz that's already full of berry notes is a treat.

berry ice cubes (make by placing
   a blueberry or strawberry into each
   hole of an ice cube tray, cover
   with water and freeze until solid)
15 ml/½ oz basil syrup (see method)
2 teaspoons freshly squeezed
   lemon juice
200 ml/¾–1 cup medium-sweet
   sparkling rosé wine

SERVES 1

Half-fill a large wine glass with berry ice cubes. Add the basil syrup and lemon juice, top up with sparkling rosé wine and stir to mix. Garnish with a basil sprig and fresh berries and serve at once.

BASIL SYRUP
Combine 250 ml/1 cup water, 225 g/1 cup sugar and a large handful of fresh basil leaves in a small saucepan. Bring to the boil, remove from the heat and let sit for 30 minutes. Strain into a screw-top jar and discard the leaves. Refrigerate and use within 2 days as it will quickly discolour.

Blooming Lovely

Orange blossom extract has an indefinable flavour that isn't exactly floral, so it adds intrigue to this elegant spritzer. Use a pink Champagne, if liked.

4 dashes of Peychaud's bitters
15 ml/½ oz St-Germain elderflower
   liqueur
¼ teaspoon orange blossom extract
½ teaspoon sugar syrup
120 ml/4 oz well-chilled Champagne
lemon zests
edible flowers, to garnish

SERVES 1

Pour the bitters, elderflower liqueur, orange blossom extract and sugar syrup into a small wine glass and add a few ice cubes. Top up with Champagne, squeeze the lemon zests over the drink and discard. Stir, garnish with an edible flower and serve at once.

Stout & Steadfast

Whilst gin and beer may seem like an odd combination, it is well-rooted in the spirit's history. The Purl was a mix of gin, ale, sugar and spices dating from Shakespeare's time and a popular early morning drink for labourers, giving them fortification for the day. It also makes the perfect refresher!

20 ml/³/₄ oz gin
20 ml/³/₄ oz rosé vermouth
20 ml/³/₄ oz Campari
60 ml/2 oz Guinness (dark Irish stout)
a splash of well-chilled Champagne
an orange slice, to garnish

SERVES 1

Add the first four ingredients to an ice-filled half-pint glass and gently stir. Add a splash of Champagne, garnish with an orange slice and serve at once.

Run Naked

A slightly lighter drink, this recipe calls for apple cider instead of stout.

25 ml/1 oz gin
25 ml/1 oz Campari
25 ml/1 oz red vermouth
300 ml/12 oz dry sparkling (hard) cider
a lime wheel or wedge, to garnish

SERVES 1

Add the ingredients (except the cider) to a salt-rimmed, ice-filled pint glass and stir. Top up with chilled cider. Garnish with a lime wheel or wedge and serve at once.

Sangria Blanca

This peachy little number will get the fiesta started. Get out all your best cocktail 'furniture' – this is no time to be tasteful.

¼ ripe peach or nectarine, skin on
10 ml/¼ oz freshly squeezed lemon juice
25 ml/1 oz golden rum
15 ml/½ oz peach schnapps
25 ml/1 oz peach juice
well-chilled Prosecco, to top up

SERVES 1

Thinly slice the peach and put it with the lemon juice, rum, peach schnapps and peach juice into a collins glass and stir well. Add a handful of ice cubes and top with Prosecco. Stir very gently, add your adornments and serve.

La Rossa

Summer in a glass. All you need is a picnic blanket, a secluded meadow and someone rather lovely to snuggle up to.

4 fresh strawberries
1 teaspoon sugar
25 ml/1 oz limoncello
1 teaspoon strawberry bursting bubbles (optional), see page 4
well-chilled Prosecco, to top up

SERVES 1

Hull three of the strawberries and chop them. Put in a cocktail shaker with the sugar and muddle until the juices are released. Add the limoncello, half-fill the shaker with ice cubes and shake. Strain into a chilled flute glass. Add the bursting bubbles, if using. Half-fill the glass with Prosecco, stir, and then top up. Slice the remaining strawberry and use it to garnish. Serve at once.

Moscow Mule

Ginger beer is what gives a mule its spiciness and it works well here with zesty lime to create the perfect refreshment for a hot day. (Pictured left.)

50 ml/1²/₃ oz vodka
1 lime, quartered
chilled spicy ginger beer,
** to top up**

SERVES 1

Add the vodka to a copper tankard or highball glass filled with crushed ice. Squeeze over the lime wedges and drop the spent husks in too. Top up with ginger beer, stir gently and serve at once.

Strawberry Mule

Break the ice with this fruitier version of the classic Moscow Mule (see recipe above).

2 thin slices of peeled
** fresh ginger**
4 fresh strawberries
50 ml/1²/₃ oz vodka
15 ml/¹/₂ oz crème de
** fraise de bois**
** (strawberry liqueur)**
a dash of sugar syrup
chilled spicy ginger beer,
** to top up**
a lime zest, to garnish

SERVES 1

Put the fresh ginger and three strawberries in a cocktail shaker and crush with a muddler. Add the vodka, crème de fraise and sugar syrup. Add a handful of ice cubes, shake sharply and strain into an ice-filled highball glass. Top up with ginger beer and stir gently. Garnish with the remaining strawberry and a lime zest and serve at once.

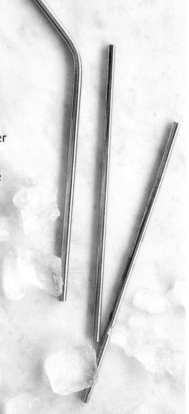

Raspberry & Lime Rickey

This is a light cocktail that is both fresh and fruity, with a sweet taste of raspberries and a hint of lime.

6 fresh raspberries
50 ml/1²/₃ oz raspberry vodka
20 ml/²/₃ oz freshly squeezed
  lime juice
chilled club soda, to top up
a lime wedge, to garnish

SERVES 1

Gently muddle five of the raspberries in the bottom of a highball glass. Fill the glass with cracked ice, add the vodka and lime juice and top up with club soda. Stir gently, garnish with a lime wedge and the remaining raspberry and serve at once.

Blackberry & Basil Mojito

A twist on the popular Mojito (see page 67), this fragrant cocktail replaces the rum with vodka and the mint with fresh basil.

4 fresh basil leaves
6 fresh blackberries
45 ml/1¹/₂ oz vodka
sparkling lemon soda, such
  as San Pellegrino Limonata,
  to top up
a small sprig of fresh basil,
  to garnish

SERVES 1

Put the basil leaves and four blackberries in the bottom of a rocks glass and gently muddle. Half fill the glass with cracked ice, add the vodka and stir, top up with lemon soda and stir again. Garnish with the remaining two blackberries and a small sprig of basil leaves and serve at once.

Rojito

The mint gives this pimped-up Mojito an unbeatable tongue-tingling freshness.

3 fresh mint sprigs, rinsed and patted dry, plus an extra sprig to garnish
2 teaspoons light brown sugar
½ teaspoon crushed pink peppercorns, plus an extra pinch to garnish
175 ml/¾ cup dry rosé wine
chilled club soda, to top up

SERVES 1

Add the mint sprigs to a cocktail shaker with the sugar and the pink peppercorns. Muddle until the mint is crushed and the liquid has been extracted. Strain into a tumbler and pour in the wine. Stir and add ice cubes. Top up with club soda then garnish with a mint sprig and a few crushed pink peppercorns. Add a straw and serve at once.

Rum 'n' Rosé on the Rocks

This laid-back drink has a distinct feel of the Deep South, worthy of sipping on any porch swing on a balmy summer night.

30 ml/1 oz dark rum
15 ml/½ oz rosé vermouth
75 ml/2½ oz bottled peach juice
50 ml/1¾ oz fruity rosé wine
1–2 teaspoons sugar syrup, to taste (optional)
chilled club soda, to top up
a slice of fresh peach and a fresh mint sprig, to garnish

SERVES 1

Put a rocks glass in the freezer for five minutes to frost. Remove it from the freezer and fill with ice cubes. Add the rum, rosé vermouth, peach juice and rosé wine to the glass. Stir to mix and then add 1–2 teaspoons of sugar syrup to taste. Garnish with a slice of fresh peach and a fresh mint sprig. Serve at once.

Lagerita

This cocktail combines two of the most refreshing beverages – beer and a Margarita – with fantastic results. Perfect for quenching your thirst on a hot summer's day by the beach.

35 ml/1¼ oz tequila
25 ml/¾ oz freshly squeezed
   lime juice
20 ml/⅔ oz agave nectar
Mexican lager, to top up

SERVES 1

Combine all the ingredients in a sling glass over crushed ice. Churn all the ingredients with a bar spoon for around 10–15 seconds, until well mixed and serve at once.

Mezcal Mule

A great example of a 'twisted classic' here – in this variation on the Moscow Mule (see page 101) mezcal marries beautifully with the lime and ginger. A cooling drink to enjoy at a midsummer's barbecue.

50 ml/1⅔ oz mezcal
15 ml/½ oz freshly squeezed
   lime juice (save a lime husk
   for garnish)
a pinch of sea salt
ginger beer, to top up
a fresh mint sprig, to garnish

SERVES 1

Add all the drink ingredients to a copper mule mug over ice cubes. Use a bar spoon to churn the drink for 10–12 seconds. Garnish with a mint sprig and the used lime husk and serve at once.

Cucumber Cooler

This simple and elegant recipe combines a homemade cucumber-infused syrup with ice-cold rosé Cava to create a drink as welcome as a fresh breeze on a warm evening.

15 ml/½ oz cucumber syrup
  (see below)
175 ml/¾ cup well-chilled fruity
    rosé Cava
a long ribbon of cucumber,
    made using a vegetable peeler

SERVES 1

Add the cucumber syrup to the glass and top up with rosé Cava. Garnish with a long single sliver of cucumber and serve at once.

CUCUMBER SYRUP
Put 250 ml/1 cup of water in a small saucepan with 225 g/1 cup white granulated sugar. Bring to the boil and simmer for a minute until clear and slightly thickened. Take off the heat and add the chopped flesh and skin of about half a medium cucumber. Leave to cool and transfer to a clean screw-top jar. Refrigerate (for a few hours or overnight if possible) to marinate, then strain the syrup, discard the cucumber pieces, and return the syrup to the jar. The syrup will keep in the fridge for up to 3 weeks.

Sparkling Berry Caipirinha

A caipirinha is THE summer drink. The eye-watering sharpness of the limes is thrilling and pleasure lies in trying to drain every last sugary sip from the glass.

8 fresh raspberries, plus 1 extra to garnish
1¹/₂–2 teaspoons raw cane sugar
¹/₂ a lime, cut into 4 wedges
30 ml/1 oz cachaça
60–90 ml/2–3 oz well-chilled Prosecco
  or rosé Prosecco, as preferred

SERVES 1

Combine the raspberries, sugar and lime in a rocks glass and muddle the raspberries with a muddler until smashed. Fill with crushed ice, pour over the cachaça and stir. Top up with Prosecco, add more crushed ice and stir. Garnish with a raspberry, add a straw and serve at once.

The Black Rose

A refreshing twist on a Caiprikoska, this is both tart and fruity, thanks to the dry rosé wine floated over sweet muddled berries and a splash of vodka.

3–4 juicy blackberries, plus 1 extra
  to garnish
1 teaspoon raw cane sugar
freshly squeezed juice of 1 lime
20 ml/³/₄ oz vodka
100 ml/3¹/₃ oz pale, dry sparkling
  rosé wine
a lime wheel, to garnish

SERVES 1

Put the blackberries and sugar in a rocks glass and muddle with a muddler or end of a wooden rolling pin until the berries are crushed. Add the lime juice. Tip in a few scoops of crushed ice, then pour over the vodka and wine. Stir once and top up with another scoop of crushed ice. Garnish with a blackberry and lime wheel, add straws and serve at once.

Rosa-rita

A delicious twist on a Margarita with an unexpected hint of spicy heat.

2 large chunks of watermelon flesh
1 small slice of fresh red chilli/
  chile, deseeded
35 ml/1¼ oz gold tequila
15 ml/½ oz rosemary syrup (see right)
20 ml/¾ oz pink grapefruit juice
1 teaspoon freshly squeezed lime juice
a splash of very sweet, fruity sparkling
  rosé wine
a small watermelon wedge, red chilli/
  chile slice and rosemary sprig
  threaded onto an olive pick, to garnish

SERVES 1

Put the watermelon and chilli/chile in a cocktail shaker and muddle. Add the tequila, rosemary syrup and both juices and shake. Strain into a rocks glass filled with crushed ice. Top up with rosé, add the garnish and a straw and serve at once.

ROSEMARY SYRUP
Put 250 ml/1 cup water in a small saucepan with 225 g/1 cup white sugar. Bring to the boil and simmer until clear and slightly thickened. Take off the heat and add 3 sprigs of fresh rosemary. When cool, strain, discard the rosemary and pour the mixture into a screw-top jar. It will keep in the fridge for up to 3 weeks.

Pinkie Swizzle

The rum swizzle is reinvented as a sparkling, ice-cold, lip-tingling treat.

40 ml/1½ oz 100% pomegranate juice
30 ml/1 oz Bacardi or other white rum
10 ml/¼ oz sugar syrup
60 ml/2 oz rosé Prosecco, well-chilled
pomegranate seeds, to garnish

SERVES 1

Combine the pomegranate juice, rum and syrup in a cocktail shaker with ice cubes and shake until chilled. Strain into a rocks glass filled with crushed ice and pour in the Prosecco. Garnish with pomegranate seeds, add a straw and serve at once.

Pitchers & Punches

Maui Punch

Captain Cook first discovered the pineapple in Hawaii in 1778. Very soon it was a staple in punch bowls across America. It lends a hint of the exotic and a soft caramel sweetness that works with most spirits. (Pictured left.)

4 pineapples, peeled, cored and sliced
450 g/1 lb superfine/caster sugar
250 ml/1 cup dark Jamaican rum
250 ml/1 cup Cognac
150 ml/²/₃ cup orange Curaçao
150 ml/²/₃ cup freshly squeezed
   lemon juice
4 x 750-ml bottles Champagne

SERVES 10

Put the pineapple slices in a large punch bowl. Sprinkle over the sugar and leave to stand, overnight if possible, until the sugar has soaked into the pineapple slices.

After this time, add the rum, Cognac, Curaçao, lemon juice and Champagne to the punch bowl along with a block of ice. Stir gently to mix and serve at once in punch cups or glasses.

Fish House Punch

This is the official punch of the oldest club in America, the Schuylkill Fishing Company. Its strength was and is legendary. If you want to bring down the strength, let it sit on the ice for a while to dilute it a little.

250 ml/1 cup freshly squeezed
   lemon juice
100 g/¹/₂ cup superfine/caster sugar
500 ml/2 cups dark Jamaican rum
250 ml/1 cup Cognac
30 ml/1 oz peach brandy
500 ml/2 cups sparkling mineral water
pared lemon zest, to garnish

SERVES 10

Put the lemon juice and sugar in a large punch bowl and stir until the sugar is dissolved. Add the remaining ingredients to the bowl along with a large block of ice, and stir gently to mix. Garnish with strips of lemon zest and serve at once in punch cups or glasses.

Regent's Punch

Also known as the George IV punch, with the addition of Champagne, this makes a great party punch, served from a classic bowl. (Pictured right.)

600 ml/2¹/₃ cups Earl Grey tea
pared zest of 3 lemons
pared zest of 1 orange
200 g/1 cup caster/superfine sugar
250 ml/1 cup Cognac
150 ml/²/₃ cup dark Jamaican rum
250 ml/1 cup freshly squeezed
  lemon juice
250 ml/1 cup fresh pineapple juice
1 x 750-ml bottle Champagne

SERVES 10

Make up the Earl Grey tea and add the lemon and orange zests and sugar whilst still hot. Stir and set aside to cool. When cooled, add to a large punch bowl with the Cognac, rum and lemon and pineapple juices. Stir gently to mix and add a large block of ice. Top up with the Champagne and serve at once, in punch cups or glasses.

Berry Collins

A deliciously fruity twist on the cocktail party classic that is the Tom Collins. (Pictured on page 5, top left.)

500 ml/2 cups London dry gin
250 ml/1 cup freshly squeezed
  lemon juice
125 ml/¹/₂ cup any fresh red berry purée
125 ml/¹/₂ cup sugar syrup
1 litre/4 cups club soda, to top up
seasonal fresh fruit, to garnish

SERVES 10

Add all the ingredients except the club soda to a pitcher or punch bowl filled with ice and stir gently to mix. Top up with soda and stir again. Serve at once in tall ice-filled glasses, garnished with seasonal fresh fruit.

Paloma Punch

Paloma translates as dove, although why this drink is so-called is a mystery! Although it may seem a lot of effort, do try, where possible, to use freshly squeezed grapefruit juice for a perfect summer freshness. (Pictured left.)

500 ml/2 cups reposado tequila
100 ml/1/3 cup agave syrup
1.5 litres/6 cups freshly squeezed
　grapefruit juice
60 ml 1/4 cup freshly squeezed
　lime juice
250 ml/1 cup club soda
salt, for rimming the glasses

SERVES 10

Put the tequila, agave syrup and grapefruit juice in a pitcher filled with ice. Squeeze the limes into the pitcher and drop the husks in too, reserving one for preparing the glasses. Top up with the soda water and stir gently to mix.

To prepare the glasses, pour some salt onto a plate. Rub the rim of the glasses with the spent lime husk. Turn each glass upside down and place it in the salt so that it coats the rim.

Fill the salt-rimmed glasses with ice, top up with punch and serve at once.

Kentucky Mule

A variation on the Moscow Mule, this twist has bourbon as the base spirit, which offers a little bit more flavour than the traditional vodka and combines beautifully with spicy ginger beer and aromatic Angostura bitters.

300 ml/1 1/4 cups bourbon
1 litre/4 cups sparkling ginger beer
6 dashes of Angostura bitters
3 limes, each cut into 8 wedges

SERVES 6

Put the bourbon, ginger beer and Angostura bitters in a large pitcher filled with ice. Squeeze the lime wedges into the pitcher and then drop the husks in too. Stir gently before serving at once in ice-filled glasses.

10 Green Bottles

Elderflower is a wonderful flavouring and Bottle Green is one of the best brands to use. It is sold globally, or should be available online. (Pictured right.)

400 ml/1²/₃ cups vodka

200 ml/³/₄ cup freshly squeezed lime juice

150 ml/²/₃ cup elderflower cordial

50 ml/scant ¹/₄ cup sugar syrup

300 ml/1¹/₄ cups pomegranate juice

300 ml/1¹/₄ cups well-chilled Prosecco

SERVES 10

Add all the ingredients to a pitcher filled with ice cubes and stir gently to mix. Serve at once in tall ice-filled glasses, garnished with the spent husks of the squeezed limes.

Watermelon Fizzy Punch

This has a natural sweetness, but the addition of cucumber and lime keeps it fresh. For teetotal guests, just replace the Prosecco with club soda.

800 g/28 oz watermelon flesh, cubed

3 small cucumbers, 1 chopped for the juice and 2 thinly sliced lengthways

1 small bunch of fresh mint, reserving some leaves to garnish

1 pink grapefruit, ¹/₂ for juice and ¹/₂ sliced into 6 rounds

3 limes, 1 sliced in rounds and 2 juiced

30 ml/2 tablespoons light agave syrup

1 x 750-ml bottle Prosecco

SERVES 6

Put the watermelon, one chopped cucumber and the mint leaves in a blender and blend together. Strain through a sieve/strainer into a pitcher. Put one slice each of grapefruit, lime and cucumber into each glass. Place the remaining sliced ingredients in the pitcher and add the grapefruit juice, lime juice and agave syrup. Mix well. Add the Prosecco and top with extra mint. Pour into ice-filled glasses and serve at once.

Pomegranate Punch

Babicka is a truly unique Czech vodka that is infused with wormwood (the key ingredient of absinthe) and which works curiously well with pomegranate. If you can't find Babicka, you can substitute your favourite vodka, flavoured or otherwise.

500 ml/2 cups Babicka vodka
750 ml/3 cups pomegranate juice
500 ml/2 cups freshly squeezed
   grapefruit juice
250 ml/1 cup freshly squeezed
   lime juice
150 ml/²/₃ cup sugar syrup
500 ml/2 cups club soda, to serve
long grapefruit zest ribbons,
   made using a vegetable peeler
   and fresh mint sprigs,
   to garnish

SERVES 10

Put the vodka, the pomegranate, grapefruit and lime juices, and the sugar syrup in a large punch bowl or pitcher filled with ice. Top up with soda water, and stir gently to mix.

Serve at once in ice-filled highball glasses, garnished with a long ribbon of grapefruit zest and sprigs of mint.

Mocktails & Cordials

Cola Cordial

You may argue that nothing quite beats the real thing, but there's something rewarding about sipping smugly on your homemade version. (Pictured left.)

200 g/1 cup white granulated sugar
200 g/1 cup dark muscovado sugar
1 vanilla pod/bean
1 cinnamon stick
a pinch of ground nutmeg
pared zest of 1 orange, 1 lemon
   and 1 lime
200 ml/³/₄ cup club soda, per serving
pared citrus zests, to garnish

MAKES ABOUT 200 ML/³/₄ CUP

Put both the sugars and 500 ml/2 cups of water in a large saucepan set over medium heat. Simmer gently, stirring frequently, until the sugar has dissolved. Turn down the heat and add the vanilla pod/bean, cinnamon, nutmeg and the zests of the citrus fruit. Allow to simmer for 2 hours over a low heat, stirring occasionally, until it has reduced to a thin syrup. Let cool and then pass though a sieve/strainer. Add the amount of cordial to suit your taste to a highball glass, dilute with soda, garnish with a citrus zest and serve at once.

Root Beer Float

This much-loved kids' drink is now all grown up! (Pictured on page 126.)

4 tablespoons sassafras extract
1 tablespoon runny honey
60–100 g/¹/₃–¹/₂ cup brown sugar
5 cloves and 12 peppercorns
5-cm/2-in piece of fresh ginger,
   peeled
club soda and vanilla ice cream,
   to serve

SERVES 4

Combine all the ingredients in a saucepan with 500 ml/2 cups water and simmer over a medium heat for about 15 minutes. Remove from the heat, cover and let sit for about 30 minutes. Allow the syrup to cool completely before straining through a sieve/strainer to get rid of the solids. Combine 4 tablespoons of the syrup with club soda in a highball glass and stir. Add two small scoops of ice cream to each glass and serve at once.

Tropical Punch

When making summer punches that involve whole fruits or fruit juices, always try to use the fresh fruit and juice, or blend it. (Pictured right.)

2 mangos, peeled, pitted and chopped

2 slices fresh pineapple

400 ml/1²/₃ cups freshly squeezed pink grapefruit juice

30 ml/1 oz freshly squeezed lime juice

2.5-cm/1-in piece of fresh ginger, peeled

scant 50 ml/¹/₄ cup sugar syrup

club soda, to top up

pineapple leaves, to garnish

SERVES 2

Add all the ingredients to a blender with 1 scoop of crushed ice and blitz until smooth. Pour into ice-filled glasses and top up with club soda to loosen the mixture, if required. Garnish with pineapple leaves and serve at once.

Citrus Fizz

As the name suggests, this is quite a sour drink, you may want to add a dash of sugar syrup to taste. (Pictured on page 5, top right.)

1 litre/4 cups freshly squeezed blood orange juice

250 ml/1 cup freshly squeezed pink grapefruit juice

100 ml/¹/₃ cup freshly squeezed lemon juice

8 scoops lemon sorbet

caster/superfine sugar, to taste

club soda, to top up

SERVES 6

Strain the freshly squeezed juices into a punch bowl with a small block of ice. Add the sorbet and a sprinkling of sugar and stir gently to mix. Serve at once in punch cups or glasses topped up with club soda.

Fresh Watermelon & Cinnamon Punch

Perhaps surprisingly, watermelon and cinnamon work well together! In fact, the delicate flavour of watermelon works well with many herbs and spices, including chilli/chile, mint and even rosemary.

2 large watermelons, peeled and roughly chopped
250 ml/1 cup freshly squeezed lime juice
100 ml/200 ml cinnamon syrup (see method)
club soda, to top up

SERVES 10

Put the chopped watermelon in a blender with the lime juice, cinnamon-infused syrup and 1 scoop of crushed ice. Blend until smooth. (You may have to blend the watermelon in batches if it all won't fit in the blender at once.) Pour the watermelon mixture into a punch bowl and add a block of ice. Top up with club soda, stir and serve at once.

CINNAMON SYRUP
Put 400 g/2 cups sugar, a pinch of ground cinnamon and 250 ml/1 cup water in a saucepan set over low heat. Heat gently, stirring until the sugar has dissolved. Remove from the heat and leave to stand for at least 2 hours before using. The syrup will keep in the fridge for up to 3 weeks.

Lemon-lime Soda

This refreshing homemade soda combines citrus and sugar with club soda, making a drink very similar to sparkling lemonade. Try adding a few mint leaves to serve for extra refreshment on a hot day.

**400 g/2 cups caster/
   supefine sugar
2 limes, sliced
2 lemons, sliced
club soda, to serve**

SERVES 4–6

In a medium saucepan, combine the sugar, lemons and limes with 450 ml/2 cups water. Bring to the boil over a medium heat and boil for 5 minutes. Remove from the heat and let cool, then pass through a sieve/strainer. To serve, dilute 1–2 tablespoons of the syrup with 250 ml/ 1 cup of club soda. Add ice cubes and serve at once.

Strawberry Soda

This delicous homemade strawberry syrup beats anything you can buy. Top up with soda for a refreshing drink, or drizzle over strawberries and cream.

**900 g/2 lb strawberries
400 g/2 cups sugar
club soda, to serve**

SERVES 4–6

Place the strawberries in a heavy-based saucepan, add 450 ml/2 cups water and bring to the boil. Stir, then reduce the heat to low and simmer for about 15 minutes, until the strawberries soften. Strain the juice into a separate saucepan, using a fine mesh sieve/strainer. Discard the strawberry pulp. Stir in the sugar until it dissolves, then bring the strawberry juice back to the boil. Reduce the heat to medium and simmer for 5 minutes. Skim any foam from the top of the syrup. Remove from the heat and let cool to room temperature. Pour the syrup into a lidded container and refrigerate. To serve, dilute 1–2 tablespoons of the syrup with 250 ml/1 cup club soda. Add ice cubes and serve at once.

Spiced Cream Soda

Cream soda is one of the most delicious, refreshing and not to mention, sweet sodas out there. This one is a spicier take on a cream soda, lending a bit of a kick to the regular cream soda flavour most of us are used to. Serve with ice cream or with spiced rum for an adult drink.

400 g/2 cups sugar
$^1/_2$ teaspoon citric acid
$^1/_2$ tablespoon molasses
1 tablespoon almond extract
1 tablespoon vanilla extract
club soda, to serve

SERVES 4–6

FRUIT & SPICE BLEND
75 g/$^1/_2$ cup dried plums/
  prunes
75 g/$^1/_2$ cup raspberries
7.5-cm/3-in piece of vanilla
  pod/bean, split
1 tablespoon juniper berries
$^1/_2$ tablespoon whole cloves
6 star anise
1 teaspoon ginger paste
1 teaspoon ground nutmeg
$^1/_2$ teaspoon ground
  cardamom
$^1/_2$ teaspoon ground
  cinnamon

In a saucepan, combine the fruit and spice blend ingredients with 450 ml/2 cups water. Bring to the boil, then remove from the heat and let steep for 30–60 minutes.

Strain out the solid ingredients and return the water to the saucepan. Add the sugar, citric acid and molasses and heat until dissolved. Remove the syrup from the heat. Chill the syrup and add the almond and vanilla extracts.

To serve, dilute 1–2 tablespoons of the syrup with 250 ml/1 cup club soda. Add ice cubes and a straw and serve at once.

Elderflower Cordial

Alcohol-free sparkling wine is widely available. Try it with this homemade cordial for an elegant glass of summer fizz.

10 elderflower heads
grated zest and freshly
   squeezed juice of 2 lemons,
   plus extra juice to taste
2 litres/quarts just-boiled
   water
500 g/2½ cups white
   granulated sugar
alcohol-free sparkling wine
   or club soda, to serve
MAKES ABOUT 2 LITRES/QUARTS

In a large heatproof container, place the elderflower heads, lemon zest and juice. Pour the just-boiled water into the container, covering them. Use a saucepan lid to hold the flower heads under the water. Leave to infuse for at least 2 hours. Line a sieve/strainer with fine muslin/cheesecloth. Pour the mixture through the lined sieve/strainer into another saucepan. Do this in batches if you don't have a big enough pan. When it has finished draining, bring the liquid to a simmer and add the sugar, dissolving it all to make the cordial. Check the flavour and add a little extra lemon juice, if needed, before decanting into sterilized bottles. Seal and cool.

To serve, add 1–2 tablespoons of the cordial to flute glasses and top up with sparkling non-alcoholic wine or club soda. Serve at once.

Blueberry Cordial

Blueberries have a lovely sweet flavour, so this is a great recipe for summer drinking. Try it mixed with lemonade, a classic combination.

750 g/6 cups blueberries

250 g/1¼ cups sugar

grated zest and freshly squeezed juice of 2 lemons

club soda or clear lemonade, to serve

MAKES ABOUT 1 LITRE/4 CUPS

Place all of the ingredients in a saucepan, along with 500 ml/2 cups water. Simmer for 30 minutes, then mash the ingredients to extract the flavour. Line a sieve/strainer with fine muslin/cheesecloth. Pour the mixture through the lined sieve/strainer into another saucepan (don't press or squash the ingredients, or the cordial will be cloudy). When it has finished draining, bring the liquid to a simmer, then decant into a sterilized bottle, seal and cool. To serve, add 1–2 tablespoons of the cordial to ice-filled glasses, top up with club soda or lemonade. Serve at once.

Red Berry Cordial

Bursting with goodness and flavour, the mix of raspberries and blackcurrants in this recipe is a combination that works brilliantly.

400 g/3 cups raspberries

350 g/3½ cups blackcurrants

350 g/1¾ cups sugar

grated zest and freshly squeezed juice of 2 lemons

club soda or clear lemonade, to serve

MAKES ABOUT 1 LITRE/4 CUPS

Place all of the ingredients in a saucepan along with 500 ml/2 cups water. Bring to a low simmer for 30 minutes, then mash the ingredients to extract the flavour. Line a sieve/strainer with fine muslin/cheesecloth. Pour the mixture through the lined sieve/strainer into another saucepan (don't press or squash the ingredients, or the cordial will be cloudy). When it has finished draining, bring the liquid to a simmer, then decant into a sterilized bottle, seal and cool. To serve, add 1–2 tablespoons of the cordial to ice-filled glasses, top up with club soda or lemonade. Serve at once.

Index

Credits

RECIPE CREDITS

Julia Charles
B&B
Black Rose
Blackberry & Basil
  Mojito
Blooming Lovely
Cucumber Cooler
Elderflower Cup
Hibiscus Fizz
La Paloma
Lavender French 75
Lavender Rosé Royale
Mediterranean Sparkle
Ouzo Sunrise
Passion Star Martini
Petal
Pineapple Sangria
Pinkie Swizzle
Pom Pom
Rojito
Rosa-rita
Rum 'n' rosé on the
  Rocks
Singapore Sling
Sparkling Cosmopolitan
Sparkling Raspberry &
  Rosé Caipirinha

Jesse Estes
Bourbon Spritz
Horse's Neck with a Kick
Lagerita
Marquee
Mexican 55
Mezcal Mule
Original Sin
Under the Volcano

Mat Follas
Blueberry Cordial

Elderflower Cordial
Flavoured Gin & Tonics
Red Berry Cordial

Laura Gladwin
Appleblack
Aviation Royale
Bellini
Bello Marcello
Beretta 18
Breakfast in Milan
Cherry Baby
Classic Champagne
  Cocktail
Coco Mango
Jalisco Flower
Jasmine Blossom
La Dolce Vita
La Passeggiata
La Rossa
Liaison Dangereuse
Lillet de Loire
Mango Morning
Mimosa
Posy
Prima Donna
Prosecco Mary
Raspberry Dazzler
Rosebud
Rosy Glow
Sangria Blanca
Sanguinello Fizz
Sparkling Manhattan
Stiletto
Tequila Sparkle
The Metropolis
Ultra Violet
Viva España

Carol Hilker
Lemon-lime Soda
Strawberry Soda

Root Beer Float
Spiced Cream Soda

Kathy Kordalis
Pomini
Watermelon Fizzy Punch

Louise Pickford
Strawberry Mule

Ben Reed
10 Green Bottles
Bay Breeze
Citrus Fizz
Cosmo Royale
Fish House Punch
Fresh Watermelon &
  Cinnamon Punch
Cola Cordial
Kentucky Cooler
Kentucky Mule
Maui Punch
Mojito
Moscow Mule
Paloma Punch
Peach Blossom Spring
Pomegranate Punch
Regent's Punch
Raspberry & Lime Rickey
Berry Collins
Tropical Punch

**David T. Smith
& Keli Rivers**
Negroni Bianco
  Bergamotto
Newbie Negroni
Porch-drinking Negroni
Run Naked
Stout & Steadfast
Sunshine Negroni
The Negroni Cup

PHOTOGRAPHY CREDITS

All images (including
front jkt & spine) by
Alex Luck, with the
following exceptions:

Peter Cassidy
Page 126

Mowie Kay
Page 115

William Lingwood
Pages 5 (top l&r), 70, 114,
  116, 119, 121, 123, 124,
  129, 131, 132

David Munns
Page 133

Steve Painter
Pages Back jacket, 90,
  138, 144

Toby Scott
Pages 135, 136

Clare Winfield
Page 102